A Grisly History of Nottinghamshire
in 10 Spine-Chilling Chapters

Michael Cox

Illustrations by
Clive Goddard

Nottinghamshire
County Council

© Text copyright Michael Cox 2011

© Illustrations copyright Clive Goddard 2011

All rights reserved. No part of this publication may be reproduced, stored or introduced into a retrieval system or transmitted in any form or by any means (electronic, mechanical, photocopy, recording or otherwise) without permission from the publishers.

Whilst every care has been taken to ensure the accuracy of the information contained in this publication, Nottinghamshire County Council cannot accept responsibility for any error or omission.

The views and opinions expressed in this publication are those of the author and do not necessarily reflect those of the publisher.

ISBN: 978-0-902751-72-9

Printed and designed by: Nottinghamshire County Council, Design and Print

CONTENTS

INTRODUCTION

CHAPTER ONE
A GRISLY NOTTINGHAMSHIRE TIMELINE — 7

CHAPTER TWO
CARNAGE AT CRESWELL — 12

CHAPTER THREE
SNOTTA SAILS UPPA THE WATTA — 15

CHAPTER FOUR
RAMBLES AROUND THE SHAMBLES — 19

CHAPTER FIVE
GOTCHA! — 27

CHAPTER SIX
THE GOOD STUFF!
(AND NOT IN THE SLIGHTEST BIT GRISLY) — 31

CHAPTER SEVEN
ALL TIED UP IN NOTTS — 38

CHAPTER EIGHT
FROM PEACEFUL, PICTURESQUE AND PASTORAL TO PUTRID, PONGY AND POISONOUS - in just a few short years! — 43

CHAPTER NINE
GRISLY NOTTINGHAMSHIRE: ROUGH AND ROWDY AND ODD AND ECCENTRIC! — 48

CHAPTER TEN
BATTERED AND BOMBED ... BUT NOT BEATEN: NOTTINGHAMSHIRE DURING THE WORLD WARS — 53

Important note

This book is essentially about the county of Nottinghamshire, which Nottingham is part of. And, until relatively recently, Nottinghamshire was loads bigger, coming right up to the edges of the old town, meaning that places like Wollaton, Clifton and St Ann's were actually in the county.

Introduction

You are about to discover the **real** history of Nottinghamshire. But first a warning! In this book please do not expect to read sloppy stories of laughing, golden-hearted hoodies robbing the rich and giving to the poor. Yes, those tales of merry medieval nitwits playing hide-and-seek in Sherwood Forest are fun! But, they're also a load of sentimental tosh! The story of the real Nottinghamshire is far more exciting and interesting than that. And, about **ten thousand** times more grisly! Yes, this seriously grizzled and battered county has got form! Plus a very **grisly** past. As you will now discover! In the following pages you will find out...

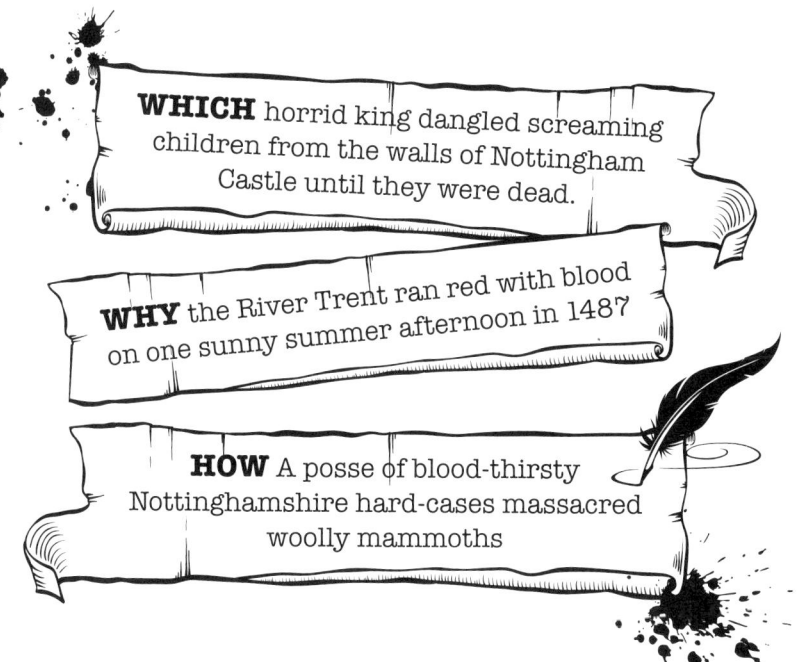

WHICH horrid king dangled screaming children from the walls of Nottingham Castle until they were dead.

WHY the River Trent ran red with blood on one sunny summer afternoon in 1487

HOW A posse of blood-thirsty Nottinghamshire hard-cases massacred woolly mammoths

WHO swallowed so many pins that she ended up looking like a human hedgehog!

WHERE you could see savage dogs ripping an enraged bear to pieces

WHICH Nottinghamshire town was blasted to bits in three bloody sieges then devastated by a grisly plague!

WHY people in Nottingham's old Market Square stuck hot ginger up horses' bottoms

WHERE Nottinghamshire farmers' fields were littered with human body bits after the most devastating explosion in the whole of World War One

plus lots, lots more ...

And, of course, amongst the grisly stuff, you'll also find out a lot of very impressive, admirable, inspiring and reassuring things about Nottinghamshire. But first, just to let you in gently, and to give you a tiny taste of what you're in for, check out ....

Chapter One

A GRISLY NOTTINGHAMSHIRE TIMELINE

Pre 40,000 BC: There are no people in Nottinghamshire, just trees and wild beasts which spend most of their time trying to kill each other (the wild beasts, not the trees).

Between 40,000 BC and 15,000 BC: Rough and uncouth prehistoric foreigners move into caves at Creswell Crags and set about slaughtering the local wildlife with absolutely no thought for the ecological impact of their actions.

6th Century: Dozens of slightly less rough and uncouth foreigners called Anglo-Saxons settle on a hill overlooking the River Trent. Their leader, the romantically named, 'Snotta', calls his exciting new housing development Snotta Inga Ham.

Late 9th Century: A bunch of ferocious fungus-faced yobs (also foreigners) called Vikings duff up the Anglo-Saxons and take over Nottingham.

920 AD: The Anglo-Saxons, now known as the 'English', recapture Nottingham from the Vikings led by King Edward the Elder, who also orders the first ever bridge to be built over the Trent (and is given a free bus-pass for his trouble). Nottingham now has a population of *hundreds!*

1066-67 AD: Yet more rough types from abroad, the Normans, thrash the living daylights out of the English at the Battle of Hastings and their leader, William the Conqueror becomes king. He has a wooden fort built at Nottingham. The town's population is now 1,500- that's about the number of pupils in an average size modern-day secondary school. In the Nottinghamshire countryside, farms grow into hamlets then into picturesque little villages such as Radford, Sneinton and Hyson Green.

1156-1170 AD: King Henry II has the castle rebuilt in stone and orders a new bridge to be built over the Trent. He calls it the Heth Beth Bridge.

1343 AD: Sir Nicholas de Cantilupe, the mega-powerful baron who lives at Greasley Castle near Moorgreen, pays for a monastery to be built in his hunting forest at nearby Beauvale. A prior and twelve monks live at Beauvale Priory spending their days praying and quietly growing vegetables.

1346 AD: Goose Fair is cancelled because of the Black Death.

1348-49: A whopping 3,000 people now live in Nottingham! However, half of them inconsiderately die during the Black Death so the population drops to 1,500. Most Nottinghamsters know each other by sight, if not by name. On market days the population increases as hundreds of people flood into town from all over Nottinghamshire to buy and sell chickens, horses, cows, pigs, shoes, stockings, pottery, tools, cheese, bread, meat, timber, candles (and eco-friendly hair conditioner).

1487 AD: The River Trent runs red with blood when no less than 4,000 soldiers are slaughtered at the battle of East Stoke near Newark-on-Trent.

1535 AD: May 5th After King Henry VIII's big falling-out with the Catholic church he seizes all the monasteries, including the one at Greasley. Five monks are dragged from Beauvale Priory then taken to London where they are hung, drawn, and quartered before having their heads stuck on stakes at the City gates (well, you can't be too careful, can you?).

1637 AD: There is now a fortnightly delivery of mail between Nottinghamshire and London. The postman walks the *entire* distance!

1642 AD: Civil War begins between King Charles I and the English Parliament. The king raises his standard at Nottingham Castle. He declares war on the Roundheads, calling on his supporters to help him to give them a slapping.

1643-1646 AD: The Nottinghamshire town of Newark-on-Trent is besieged by the Parliamentarians but finally gives up when King Charles chucks in the towel at a pub in Southwell. The Plague ravages Newark.

1660 AD: The population of Nottingham is now about 4,000 with thousands more living in Nottinghamshire's surrounding towns and villages. Lots of them earn their living making stockings, labouring on farms and working down t'pit at places like Mansfield, Eastwood and Wollaton.

1700 AD: Nottingham now has a population of about 5,000. But that's still only two-thirds as many as live in the Nottinghamshire town of Southwell today.

1801 AD: The population of Nottingham now *rockets* to 29,000 as people from all over Nottinghamshire flood into town in search of work.

1831 AD: The town's population has now shot up to 50,000 and many of them rampage around because they haven't been given the right to vote. They burn down Nottingham Castle and call the toffs rude names.

1914 AD: Nottingham has grown like crazy - there are now an astonishing 250,000 people living here. Britain's first modern police force is pounding the beat, trams are clanking around the streets, industries like Players Cigarettes, Raleigh Bicycles, Shipstones Brewery and Boots the Chemist are set up - people can now cycle to work whilst boozing and smoking a fag then have their wounds plastered as they're arrested for crashing into a tram.

2011 AD: There are now a mind-boggling 780,000 people living in Nottinghamshire and another 300,000 in Nottingham. What ever would old Snotta make of that!

Chapter Two

CARNAGE AT CRESWELL

As you can see, grisly Nottinghamshire has been around for absolutely ages, including the Paleolithic Age, the Bronze Age, the Iron Age, (the Awkward Age) and many, many more. At first it didn't have any human beings, so for about 160 million years, it was only very *slightly* grisly: sauropods menacing clumps of lichen, the odd pterodactyl ripping the guts out of giant dragonflies, that sort of thing. But then, those cantankerous, crazy, but consistently creative animals known as human beings arrived and, quite inevitably, things began to get *really* grisly! As you will now discover ...

**The place: Creswell Crags,
           Nottinghamshire**
The time: 15,000 BC

The scene: It is daybreak and mist rises from a glassy lake. Birds of prey circle overhead shrieking mournfully. Occasionally, large brown fish break the surface of the lake. Caves are visible in the limestone cliff face which is reflected in the water. Inside them, flames flicker and figures move. As the sun appears above the distant hills, men emerge from the caves. They are clad in animal skins and carry fearsome-looking clubs and spears. They scramble up a steep path and move silently and purposefully through the frozen undergrowth. Birds twitter in alarm and small animals scurry for safety. The men quickly cover several miles and finally reach a rocky outcrop overlooking a deep ravine. They gather briefly, whisper intently, then set off in different directions, crouching low. The birds and small animals fall silent.

A mile or so from the creeping men, a gigantic bull mammoth raises its massive head and sniffs the morning air. Surrounding the bull are female mammoths and their calves. They graze peacefully, unaware of the terrible fate which is about to befall them. Close to the mammoths, stacks of brushwood form a crude corridor leading to the nearby ravine.

All at once the silence is broken by the trumpeting of the bull mammoth. It has sensed danger. But too late. The screaming men are already charging the herd, hurling rocks and spears. Simultaneously, the piles of brushwood are set alight. As one, the insanely trumpeting mammoths begin a headlong stampede towards the ravine. But things are not entirely in the hunters' favour. One of them stumbles. The bull turns and charges him, its enormous tusk penetrating his chest and emerging from his back. As blood bubbles from his screaming mouth, the bull lifts him high in the air, dashes him to the ground and stamps him to a bloody mush.

The rest of the mammoths are almost at the ravine. Unable to halt their headlong charge they begin to tumble over the edge. Soon, the ravine is filled with dead and dying mammoths, their smashed limbs twisted grotesquely. Their screams of agony are now accompanied by the triumphant yells of the hunters who are already amongst them, hacking savagely at their living flesh. They are quickly joined by their women and children. Soon, all of them are grunting and laughing with pleasure as they shove fistfuls of raw meat into their bloody mouths. Welcome to grisly Nottinghamshire.

Chapter Three

SNOTTA SAILS UPPA THE WATTA

Of course, back in those far off times, Nottinghamshire wasn't called Nottinghamshire, and the place we now call Nottingham, which the county is named after, wasn't called Nottingham. However, as time passed, and human beings began to develop that 'must-have' newfangled skill known as language, they got into the habit of wanting to give a name to absolutely everything they encountered. So, around 600 BC, give or take a weekend or three, some bright spark decided to call Nottingham, Tig Guocobac, which means the Place of Cave Dwellings. But humans, being the vain and arrogant creatures they are, it wasn't long before some jumped-up little barbarian decided to name the place after himself!

ARE WE THERE YET, DAD?

A playlet

It's a cold and rainy Tuesday afternoon sometime during the 6th century AD. Anglo-Saxon, **Snotta***, his wife* **Bogey***, their ten snotty-nosed kids, his brother,* **Mucus***, his wife* **Gloopy***, and their kids are in a leaky old boat. They're not happy. Having been driven from their home in Saxony by even fiercer barbarians than they are, they've escaped across the North Sea and are making their way up the river we now call the Trent. They've endured storms at sea, attacks by strangers and wild animals, hunger and freezing cold.*

Snotta's kids (all together): Are we there yet, dad?

Snotta: Wajja mean, 'Are we there yet?' How am I expected to know if we're there when I don't even know where we're blinkin' well goin'.

Bogey: Well, I think it's time we stopped and dried out.

Mucus: See that big hill over there? It has an all-round view which means no one can sneak up on us. We could camp on it tonight.

Gloopy: And that forest will be full of deer and wild boar. There are also plenty of fish in this river.

Bogey: And these water meadows between here and the hill will provide good grazing for the cow. By the way, has anyone seen the cow?

Mucus: Come to think of it, I haven't. Not since we heard that big splash about half an hour ago.

Everyone: Ooer!

* * *

Five hours later. Snotta and his clan are sitting by a fire on the big hill eating barbecued boar.

Snotta, *pointing to a cave:* With a bit of timber round it, that'll be just the ticket to spend the night. I'll nip back to the boat and get me 'ammer and some nails.

Bogey: Its not there!

Snotta: What, me 'ammer?

Bogey: No, the boat!

They all look up to see their boat disappearing round a bend in the river.

Snotta *glaring at his eldest son:* Wollaton, you Saxon simpleton, I thought I told you to tie the boat up.

Wollaton: I did dad, but my knot wasn't all that good!

Snotta: Oh blithering barbarians! Now we're stuck.

Bogey: We'll just have to make the best of things, hubby. It could be worse.

Mucus: Yes, look on the bright side, bro'. We've got plenty of wood for building houses and keeping warm.

Gloopy: Plus the river for fish and fresh water!

Moo moo moo

Snotta: Who said that?

They all turn around to see their cow, dripping wet, walking up the hill.

Bogey: Well, there's bit of luck! Perhaps this place will be good for us after all.

Mucus: Maybe we'll settle and make a go of it!

Wollaton: And from now on I'll try and tie me knots better.

Snotta: Knots! Knots! I'll give you knots!

Chapter Four

RAMBLES AROUND THE SHAMBLES

So, as Snotta and his rellies got busy turning the Place of Cave Dwellings into a cutting-edge, fortified hill settlement, whilst spending all their spare moments making lots of new little 'Snottingahamsters' to live there, Snotta Inga Ham began to grow. And, in just a few hundred years, it had developed into not just *one*, but *two* settlements! One of them was the old 'English' town, which Snotta had begun and the other was a new town full of Norman French-speaking 'Pierre-come-latelys' who had settled around the wooden castle built by William the Conqueror in 1067. And the space between these towns became an enormous market place where the Normans and English would trade goods, call each other rude names, and occasionally belt the living daylights out of each other.

Now, life in 'olden times' was said to be nasty, brutish and short (and more than likely, so was your dad), so if you went for a wander around the Old Nottingham Market Place any time between 1100 and 1800 AD you would have seen some very shocking sights. Here are ten appalling things you might have witnessed on such a ramble. See if you can work out which are true and which are made up.

TEN REALLY *GRISLY THINGS* TO SEE AND DO IN THE OLD NOTTINGHAM MARKET PLACE

TRUE OR FALSE - YOU DECIDE!

1) Watch savage dogs try to tear a chained-up bear to pieces and bet on which ones will survive being ripped apart by the bear's claws (NB: the dogs don't do the betting, you do).

True — **False**

2) Listen to the screams of a woman being drowned in the horse pond as she's punished on the 'ducking stool'.

True — **False**

3) Throw stones at a tied-up cockerel until it's dead - an activity especially popular with local children (all keen members of the RSPB: Royal Society for the Persecution of Birds).

True / **False**

4) Poke a chained-up bull with a stick until it goes mad with rage then watched it being gruesomely slaughtered by a butcher from the 'Shambles' meat market.

True / **False**

5) Watch fighting cocks peck and gash each other to death. This one's also really popular with local children.

True / **False**

6) See a woman being whipped for stealing a few lumps of coal.

True / **False**

7) Watch a man dragging his wife along by rope he's tied around her neck then selling the rope for sixpence and his wife for two shillings and a pint of ale.

True / **False**

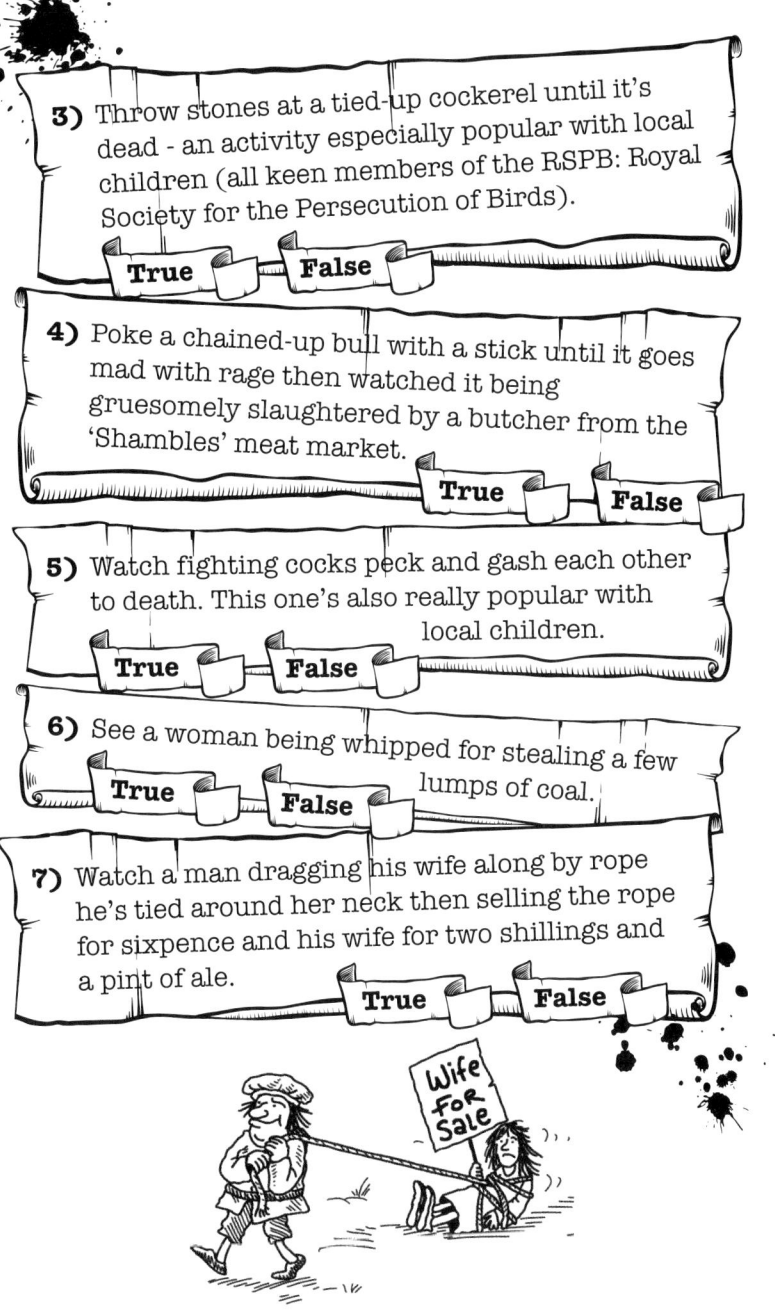

8) Hurl some dog muck at an old man locked in the pillory for trying to steal an apple (but don't forget to wash your hands afterwards).　True　False

9) Wander up to the cages on Bearward Lane and check out the miserable, flea-ridden bears which are imprisoned in them as they await their 'baiting'.　True　False

10) See a 'Shambles' butcher dragged around the market place then put in the pillory for trying to sell maggoty meat. Now see that same meat being burned under his nose.　True　False

But the market place wasn't all grisliness. There were several slightly less shocking things to do. Nevertheless, you still had to beware of all the dodgy market traders. And health and safety wasn't all it should have been either!

ANSWERS: ALL TRUE!

THREE SLIGHTLY LESS *GRISLY THINGS* TO DO IN THE OLD MARKET PLACE

1) Buy a bear mug as a souvenir of the gruesome bear-baiting you just watched.

2) Buy a live goose. There are plenty to choose from as no less than 20,000 of these bird-brains strut their way from Lincolnshire to the autumn 'Goose Fair'. Imagine the noise! Their feet are coated with tar so that they don't wear away. They're accompanied by goose-girls and goose-boys whose job it is to ensure that they don't make a dash for freedom.

3) Go shopping for fresh meat, bread, pepper, oats, salted bacon, corn, lampreys, tanned hides, mackerel, coal, pigs, apples, hens, horses, carts, horse shoes, nails, woad, wool (and eco-friendly hair conditioner).

TEN THINGS TO BEWARE OF IN THE OLD MARKET PLACE

1) Loaves of bread containing stones and pieces of iron to increase their weight.

2) Pepper dampened to make it weigh more - and rot sooner!

3) Sacks containing rotting oats hidden under fresh oats.

4) The open sewer which runs between Sheep Lane (now Market Street) and Cow Lane (now Clumber Street) carrying wee, human poo, rotting vegetables, animal guts, dead dogs and worse.

5) The saw pit on Timber Hill. It's really easy to fall in, especially on dark nights.

6) The meat-flies, wild cats and rabid dogs which plague the Shambles meat market. One bite from those dogs will drive you mad before you suffer an agonising death.

7) The rotting green meat sold by crooked butchers, especially if it's been in the caves under the Shambles which are also used for storing raw sewage.

8) The huge horse-drawn carts which trundle down extremely narrow Sheep Lane or 'Blood Lane', as the locals call it. Many a pedestrian has been crushed to death by them. Check out the bloodstained walls!

9) Dealers trying to sell you worn-out old horses which are literally 'gingered up' by having a piece of hot root ginger stuck up their bottom in order to make them 'frisky'.

10) Stolen horses which have been deliberately blinded so that they can't find their way home or recognise their real owners.

What do you mean, you'd 'rather go to Tesco'?

It wasn't just the old Market Place where grisly stuff took place. Up in that big 'bully-boy' of a castle which William had built on that dirty great rock, some very grisly stuff was going on!

NOTTINGHAM CASTLE: SOME VERY GRISLY EVENTS

1140 - Massacre in the church

Robert of Gloucester and the army of Empress Matilda attacked Nottingham Castle which was held by her enemy, King Stephen. Unable to get into the castle, Robert's mob of murderous thugs turned their fury on the townsfolk, chasing them into St Peter's Church, where they tortured and massacred them before looting and burning down the whole town.

1212 - Slaughter of the Innocents

In order to keep the Welsh Prince Llewellyn under his thumb, wicked King John took 28 sons of various Welsh leaders hostage and kept the little lads prisoner in Nottingham Castle. While he was hunting in Sherwood Forest he heard that the Prince and his leaders were rising against him so him and his mates held a pow-wow under an oak tree near Edwinstowe, now known as the 'Parliament Oak'. Then, swearing "by the teeth of God" that he wouldn't eat until he'd had his vengeance, he galloped all the way back to Nottingham Castle (on his horse, of course), snatched the small boys from their games and hanged them from the Castle walls. It's said that the children's dying screams could be heard all over the town.

Another thing horrid John did at Nottingham Castle was to have some poor bloke wrapped in lead then thrown in a dungeon and left to suffocate, just because he'd decided he didn't like him.

October 1330 - Roger's 'Come-Uppance'!

Queen Isabella and her boyfriend, Roger Mortimer, were chilling out in Nottingham Castle, no doubt feeling pretty good about being rulers of England. However, the much-miffed supporters of Isabella's 15 year old son, King Edward III, crept up a 98 metre tunnel leading from the foot of Castle Rock and took them prisoner. Roger was taken to London where he was hung for a while then chopped up with his various bits and bobs left on display as warning to anyone else who might be fancying a bit of hanky-panky with the queen. The tunnel is now known as Mortimer's Hole.

Chapter Five

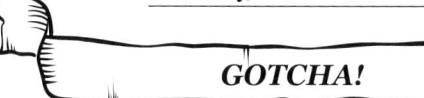

GOTCHA!

While Nottingham was undoubtedly the setting for all-round grisliness, all sorts of other horrid goings-on were also taking place in Nottinghamshire itself; mainly in the form of big, bloody battles! The biggest and bloodiest of them all happened one sunny summer's day in a beautiful bit of countryside on the banks of the sparkling River Trent.

The Trent Valley Times — 17th June 1487

THE DAY THE RIVER RAN RED!

Yesterday, the normally peaceful green meadows surrounding the sleepy little village of East Stoke near Newark-on-Trent were alive with the crash of cannon, the clash of swords and the screams of dying men. In the morning, 12,000 soldiers loyal to King Henry VII marched the eight miles from Radcliffe-on-Trent to Stoke Field where they fought a furious three hour battle with 6,000 supporters of Lambert Simnel, the boy who has been falsely crowned king.

Simnel's lot, consisting of 4,000 Irish and 2,000 German rent-a-thugs were positioned on a hill, surrounded on three sides by the river. When King Henry's troops arrived they charged down from the hill and began a battle which raged for three hours, maces crushing skulls, war-hammers splattering brains, pole-axes slicing off legs and swords piercing intestines. At one point it seemed as though Simnel's army might triumph but the Irish, almost naked (why don't they wear armour!), were soon mown down by a hail of arrows. In no time, thousands of them, looking like bloody pincushions, were writhing in agony. And, having nowhere to retreat to, the survivors had to stand their ground and fight. Soon, a torrent of blood was gushing down the ravine which leads from the field to the river, turning the waters of the Trent crimson. By the end of the morning 4,000 of Simnel's supporters had been slaughtered and he was in the hands of the victors. Long live King Henry VII!

Can't you keep a civil tongue in your head?

At least the battle of East Stoke was over in an afternoon. About two hundred years later, during the English Civil War, the townsfolk of nearby Newark-on-Trent had to put up with almost four whole years of bombardment, blood and buboes!

Cannon Balls in My Pudding Basin

Extracts from the diary of Marmaduke Fishpool Newark Bloke and Supporter of King Charles I

27th February 1643: Today 6,000 Roundheads did lay siege to Newark. Our defenders peppered their putrid Parliamentarian backsides! They are fleddeth!

12th March 1644: We are once more besieged by the poxy Parliamentarians. They bombard us day and night. Yesterday my neighbour and his three children were roasted alive when a fiery grenade did torch their thatched roof. Their screams will stay with me forever.

21st March: Huzzah! Brave Prince Rupert and his great army have rescued us. The Roundheads are once more fleddeth!

28th November 1645: Bad news. They are back. Here we goeth again!

Christmas Day 1645: We shiver, we starve, the well is frozen and the cannonballs crash down on us.

December 26th: My brother is shot. Surely things cannot become worse.

December 28th 1645: The bloody hole in my brother's chest is turned green and stinketh much. My servant, Jacob, has a fever and pink pustules cover his face. It is typhus!

January 1st 1646: My brother is dead. So is Jacob. Happy New Year (not!)

January 4th 1646: Today two soldiers came to my house and asked me for two buckets of my wee. It is to make gunpowder. I will give them three buckets of my wee. I love my King dearly and would pee this great man a whole lake of wee-wee if he asked me for it!

February 6th 1646: To stay warm I burn my furniture. Today I ate a fat rat with much relish.

27th March 1646: The streets are ankle-deep in stinking human sewage. A pig sticks its snout inside the stomach of a rotting horse.

28th April 1646: Three people all covered with dribbling buboes and with foam coming from their mouths ran down Balderton Gate today. One screamed and banged her head against a tree. And I am puking black bile. It is the plague!

6th May 1646: Yesterday our king surrendered to the Parliamentarians at Southwell. He has commanded us to surrender also. The siege of Newark is over. But the plague rages on and I am not much longer for this world.

Chapter Six

THE GOOD STUFF!
(NOT IN THE SLIGHTEST BIT GRISLY)

And now it's time for a well-earned rest from all that battling, bleeding and bashing. Nottinghamshire's not all about blood and guts. Lots of other really good stuff went on, and still does, like invention, industry, co-operation, creativity and .... lurve!

A Nottinghamshire Fairy Story
Willy ... Or Won't He?

Once upon a time a young chap called William Lee (1563-1614) went nuts about a beautiful girl who lived in his home village of Calverton in Nottinghamshire. Alas, the lovely girl was far too busy to get silly with Willy.

'All she does is knit stockings all day long!' groaned Willy. 'One of these days she'll turn into a pair of knitting needles!' And then he had his brilliant idea!

'I will invent a machine to do her knitting for her. It will imitate the movement of my true-love's hands. But instead of just two hands, it will have lots and therefore it will get the work done loads faster, thus giving my heart-throb lots of spare time for snogging and whatnot with yours truly! Ooh ooh!'

William's amazing new 'framework knitting machine' worked so well that he took it to Queen Elizabeth I herself, hoping she would allow him to make lots of them. But the queen feared that these wondrous machines would leave thousands of knitters with 'idle hands' and, as we all know, the Devil makes work for them, so she said, 'Bog off, snotty-snout!' or words to that effect.

So William took his knitting machine to France but sadly died before seeing his amazing invention become the mega-success it was destined to be. And mega-success it did become when, a hundred years or so later, thousands of framework-knitting machines were busily clattering away in the towns and villages of Nottinghamshire, making the county world-famous for its snazzy stockings, natty knickers and stylish socks. And now, all over the world, millions of knitting machines, all based on William's idea, whirr and purr, churning out billions and billions of knitted garments.

NB: Boring people say the bit of the story about William fancying the girl is a Nottinghamshire folk-tale, but the rest is most definitely true.

So, cool Nottinghamshire bloke, William, invented the world's first framework knitting machine. And that's not the only Nottinghamshire first. Here are some more ...

Nottinghamshire firsts

1604: **The first ever railway track** in England was built between Strelley and Wollaton. Horses pulled wagon loads of coal along its wooden rails.

1865: Nottinghamster, John Peake Knight, invented the **first ever traffic lights**. On 9 December 1868 John's lights were installed near Westminster Bridge in London and operated by a policeman. They were an immediate success! But then, disaster struck. One evening a leaky gas mains caused the traffic lights to explode in the face of the policeman working them, burning him badly. John's traffic light project was abandoned.

1880: **Football shin guards** were invented in Nottingham by Notts Forest player, Sam Widdowson.

1896: Frederick Gibson Garton invented **HP Brown Sauce** in his back-garden pickling factory in Basford.

September 1996: The first major **'Gut-barging' championships** were held at Rock City in Nottingham. This involved people smearing their naked fat bellies with oil then bashing them together (so who says this isn't the most sophisticated place in England).

Yes, Nottinghamshire's full of enterprising, energetic and creative people who've made their names world famous. Like these ...

Famous Nottinghamshire characters

Lord Byron 1788 – 1824

Lord Byron was a brilliant poet who liked weird animals, parties and snogging (girls, not animals). He had pet bear at university and kept ten horses, eight great big dogs, five cats (normal size), three monkeys, an eagle, a crow and a falcon at his ancestral home, Newstead Abbey. He died of fever when he went to fight in the Greek War of Independence. He's buried at Hucknall.

Sir Jesse Boot 1850 – 1931

Jesse was born in Hockley where he worked in his dad's herbalist shop. He later opened a chemist shop and sent a man round Nottingham ringing a bell and telling everyone that Boots was the cheapest chemist in town (to which everyone replied ' pull the other one, it's got bells on'). Growing richer by the minute he also bought himself an enormous mansion in The Park, where his neighbour was our next famous Nottinghamster. Boots now employs 75,000 people in 130 countries and, amongst other things, sells shed-loads of face cream, headache cures and hair conditioner.

John Player 1839 – 1884

John had a tobacco shop in Beastmarket Hill in Nottingham. In those days cancer-flakes and cancer-sticks were sold loose but John had the idea of pre-packing them and set up factories in Broad Marsh and Radford to do so. They were so successful that he was also soon able to buy himself his dirty great mansion in The Park.

Albert Ball 1896 – 1917

Albert Ball was a heroic WWI fighter pilot who was awarded the Victoria Cross for being amazingly brave. He shot down an astonishing 44 enemy fighter planes but tragically crashed to his death in 1916 whilst battling the enemy.

Alan Sillitoe 1928 – 2010

Alan Sillitoe was an author and poet who wrote books including 'The Loneliness of a Long Distance Runner' and 'Saturday Night and Sunday Morning', a novel about people living in rough-tough Radford and posh Wollaton. It is not known whether he ever owned any monkeys.

Su Pollard 1949 –

Su played chalet maid Peggy Ollerenshaw in Hi-de-Hi, a sit-com set in a British 'holiday camp' (a bit like a prisoner-of-war camp, but much less fun). She's also acted in other sit coms, made pop records and appeared in masses of pantomimes.

Herol 'Bomber' Graham 1959 –

Fleet-footed British boxer undefeated in his first 38 fights, Herol often staged shows where he invited people to hit him. But, even though he had his hands tied behind his back, they never could! Herol was very quick on his feet.

Some strange Nottinghamshire names

There were some very odd first names around in old Nottinghamshire including Reform, Vinefruite, Livewell, Frendlesse and Penitence. There was also a lawyer called Caractacus d'Aubigney Shilton and a surveyor known as Marriot Ogle Tarbotton. And when he grew up, the architect Fothergill Watson had his name changed to Watson Fothergill. Watson Fothergill designed 100 unique and beautiful buildings, many of which can still be seen in the city of Nottingham. And while we're on the subject of weird names we mustn't forget Captain Athelstan Popkess who was boss of Notts cops. Captain Popkess introduced all sorts of newfangled policing ideas including cop cars, police dogs and traffic wardens. He lived in the Park where, for reasons known only to himself, the old spoilsport banned boys from sledging down Tattershall Drive. During a trial, he recommended that a prisoner be put on probation rather than going to clink. Overwhelmed, the grateful man said, 'I would like to thank Poptin Catpiss from the heart of my bottom.'

Now ... back to the grisliness!

Chapter Seven

ALL TIED UP IN NOTTS
A (very) rough guide to crime and punishment in Nottinghamshire

Life in the bad-old, good-old days was harsh. It's said that the murder rate in the medieval ages was a shocking twelve times as high as it is now! So, just by going for a stroll around your neighbourhood, you really did take your life in your hands! And, in those cruel and unenlightened times, punishments were swift, harsh and brutal. Grisly Nottinghamshire being no exception! As these wretched Nottinghamshire wrong-doers all found out...

A Joan and three Johns
(none of them in the slightest bit honest)

1) Joan Phillips: Gobsmacked by a geezer!

Joan Phillips, farmer's daughter and seventeenth century 'ladette', was a member of the evil gang led by the villainous, Swift Nicks. Dressed in men's clothes, Joan roamed the highways of Nottinghamshire robbing and roughing-up innocent travellers. In 1685, full of bravado and testosterone, Jo galloped up to a coach on the Loughborough road, a pistol in each hand, yelling, 'Give us yer money, bacteria breath!' or something like that. However, much to her surprise, instead of handing over the mazuma, the plucky driver leapt from his coach and punched Joan in the chops so hard that she fell off her horse. Completely 'gobsmacked' by this unexpected turn of events, Joan was arrested, tried at the County Gaol then hung at the junction of Wilford Lane and Loughborough Road.

2) John Spencer: Causing a stink in Scrooby

On the night of July 3rd, 1779, John Spencer murdered William Yeadon, the keeper of the Scrooby toll-bar in north Nottinghamshire, along with his mother, Mary, so that he could steal their dosh. John was caught, found guilty and executed in Nottingham. His body was then hung in chains near Scrooby toll bar with the murder weapon, a heavy hedge-stake, in its hand. A few weeks later a soldier playfully shot several holes in John's body which caused him to begin decomposing very rapidly (John, not the soldier) and quite soon the foul odour of his putrid remains was wafting over Scrooby, causing no end of a stink.

3) John Milner: Bad noose - Good noose!

John Milner of Nottinghamshire was sentenced to hang for stealing three cows but when the trapdoor opened, the rope broke. Unfortunately for John, one of the people watching the execution was a rope maker who quickly repaired the noose, ensuring that it didn't break a second time.

4) John Henstock: Bad to the bone!

In 1815, after murderer John Henstock had been hung, the surgeons at the Nottingham General Hospital, eager to have a good 'butchers' at his bits and bobs, carefully took him to pieces. They then reassembled his skeleton and hung it from wires, obviously to remind themselves what went where when they were putting other people back together.

They didn't just hang the bad 'uns in those far-off times. They whipped them, they burned them, they branded them, they stuck them in the pillory and stocks so that the general public could chuck crud at them, and they ducked them in ponds. But when it came to combining these various punishments into natty 'one-stop suffering' devices, grisly Nottinghamshire excelled!

Grisly Nottinghamshire's first ever 'double-ducker'

There were at least four ducking stools in grisly Nottinghamshire including ones in Southwell, Newark, Retford and Nottingham. However the one in Nottingham market place was a super-duper, newfangled 'double-ducking' stool with integral pillory with room for two people and handy holes in the sides for their heads to poke through.

In 1731 the Mayor ordered a woman to be put in this contraption then left her to the mercy of the mob who all got so carried away with ducking, dissing and duffing her up that she either died of shame, duffing or drowning (come to think of it, it was most probably the last two). The Mayor was later prosecuted and the double-ducking-stool was (painlessly) destroyed.

Yapping all the way to the brank

One of the most horrid things kept in the 'naughty cupboard' at grisly Nottinghamshire's County Hall was the brank, a yucky cage-like thingy with sharp spikes designed to painfully press down on the tongue of whoever was unlucky enough to have it clamped on their head.

There was a serious shortage of feminists in the olden-days so, surprise, surprise, it was mainly women who were made to wear the brank. Having been found guilty of such utterly despicable crimes as criticising their lazy, drunken husbands, telling off Nottinghamshire yobs for anti-social behaviour, or daring to stick up for themselves against some bossy local official, the unlucky ladies were led around town on a chain, or tied to a whipping post, with the brank on their head, while all 'decent and right-thinking' Nottinghamsters jeered them and pelted them with stones, rubbish and cow-muck. And, of course, if the women attempted to speak up for themselves, the spikes caused horrible injuries to their tongue (ah, the good-old-days, how we miss them).

In 1799 a blind beggar called James Brodie was found guilty of murdering a boy in Sherwood Forest and sentenced to death. However, as he awaited his execution, the beggar made such a racket that he had the brank clamped on his head.

Sometimes one bad thing leads to another ... then another! In the mid-nineteenth century the grisly murder of an entire family was just the starting point for whole series of doom-laden disasters!

The Domino Effect

For reasons known only to himself, William Saville murdered his wife and children in Colwick Woods in 1844. A huge, blood-thirsty throng of Nottingham folk turned up to see wicked William dangle from the gallows (grisly spectacles of human degradation like 'X Factor' and 'Strictly Come Dancing' being few and far between in those days). Such was the crowd's excitement as woeful Willy thrashed and twisted, finally turning a horrid shade of purple, that the baying mob began to sway and push so much that hundreds of them tumbled down the steep steps of Garner's Hill like falling dominos. When the heap of bloodied bodies was finally untangled, thirteen of them were found to have been crushed to death (while the survivors, thankful for their good fortune, went for a cup of tea in nearby Marks and Spencers).

Chapter Eight

FROM PEACEFUL, PICTURESQUE & PASTORAL TO PUTRID, PONGY & POISONOUS - in just a few short years!

Lots of people who visited Nottinghamshire before the middle of the eighteenth century described it as a lovely place with a beautiful town at its heart. But then industry came to the county, throwing thousands of farm labourers out of work and forcing them to seek jobs in the rapidly expanding factories of the town which was becoming more unpleasant and overcrowded by the day! Read the following two letters from visitors and see just how dramatically the place deteriorated ...

Before   **After**

BEFORE: PARADISE ON EARTH!

Nottingham

May 1750

Dear friend

My travels have brought me to Nottingham and I can honestly say it is the most beautiful town in all England. Everywhere one goes there is the sound of birdsong, the baaing of sheep, the neighing of horses, the smell of apple blossom and the happy chatter of the prosperous and friendly townsfolk. Orchards, meadows and gardens are everywhere while elegant redbrick merchants' houses with tiled roofs grace the tree-lined streets. Everywhere there is a sense of space and well-being. Just to the east of the town, fat cows graze the lush water-meadows which border the sparkling Trent. To the west, the picturesque Nottinghamshire villages of Radford, Lenton, Wollaton, Bulwell and Bilborough sit amongst fields where country folk collect water from the river Leen, hoe fields or tend to their animals. Friend, I truly feel that this town and its surrounding county of Nottinghamshire is Paradise re-discovered.

Yours as ever

Watt A. Beauty

AFTER: WHAT A HELL HOLE!

London

August 1850

Your Majesty

I have just returned from Nottingham and I can honestly say it is the filthiest, most horrid place in all England! In Narrow Marsh, with its permanent stinking fog, I saw a maze of crumbling alleys and fetid courtyards containing the back-to-back slum houses in which thousands of skeleton-like men, women and children wallow in their own filth. In amongst their so-called 'houses', the throats of screaming pigs are cut and horses are butchered. For washing, cooking and drinking, hundreds of miserable human-beings share one tap for water which is swimming with sewage particles. And as for toilets! The yards simply have a wooden bench with three or four holes where men, women and children sit together, all doing their business. I not only saw human waste running over the cobbles, but through living rooms themselves. Then there is the crime! Everywhere I went, thugs lurked, waiting to beat or murder the weak and innocent for just a few pennies.

But, more than the crime, it is the squalor which affected me. No wonder more than half the children born in this hellish place die before they're five! Your Majesty, we are the richest, most powerful nation on earth. So why should our people have to live like this?

Yours respectfully
Disgusted of Tunbridge Wells

There weren't just grotty hell-holes in the town either. They also existed in Nottinghamshire in places such as Gonalston Mill at Lowdham, as a little boy called Robert Blincoe (1792-1860) found out to his cost!

A WARNING TO CHILDREN EVERYWHERE!
To whosoever should find this letter ...

My name is Robert Blincoe and this is my story. I lived my first seven years in a London Orphanage. Then, in August 1799, a fine-looking gentleman arrived and said to us, "Little ones, if you come with me to Nottinghamshire you will be taught reading and writing and be turned into little ladies and gentleman. You will dine on plum pudding and roast beef. Your pockets will jingle with cash! Who will come?"

"Me, me!" we all cried, jumping up and down with excitement. The smiling gentleman picked out 80 lucky children, including me!

The day came for us to go to Nottinghamshire. We were bundled into horse-drawn wagons, their windows heavily barred and their floors covered in straw. Then, for days, we bumped along rutted roads and soon our sick covered the straw. But no one came to clear it. Finally we arrived at a huge lace and cotton factory called Gonalston Mill at Lowdham village where we were given foul porridge and stale bread.

'Where is the plum pudding and roast beef?' I wondered.

At five o'clock the next morning a ferocious-looking man cracked a whip and set us to work in a room full of stinking, deafening machines. I was made to pick up bits of cotton. After 14 hours my back felt like it was broke. I now knew that we had been cruelly tricked and sold to the mill owners by the orphanage. Yes, we were slaves! I began to cry.

After some weeks of this torture I decided to run away. When no one was looking I slipped out of the mill and started off for London. But, when I came to a place called Bert and Joyce, a tailor who worked at the mill caught me and dragged me back. Then I was beaten black and blue. But this wasn't the worst of it. Not long after this my finger was cut off by a machine. And then my friend Mary suffered even worse when she was dragged into a machine and whirled around and around, her bones cracking and blood splashing everywhere as her head got mangled terribly. But compared to what was soon to happen to us at Litton Mill in Derbyshire, this was nothing!

Reader! Beware of smiling men who make promises which seem too good to be true. Or, like me, you will suffer terribly!

Chapter Nine

GRISLY NOTTINGHAMSHIRE ROUGH AND ROWDY AND ODD AND ECCENTRIC!

Over the centuries the good folk of Nottinghamshire have developed a reputation for general all-round stroppiness. But is it justified? Read about these six raucous riots and see what you think.

Six Savage Nottinghamshire Riots

The Great Cheese Riot - 1764: Nottingham market place: Nottingham townsfolk were so cheesed off with Nottinghamshire country folk charging such high prices for dairy products that they pinched their huge cheeses and began rolling them down Wheeler Gate (closely followed by another gang rolling giant pickled onions). The Mayor tried to intervene but was knocked over by a huge cheese (yes, the poor man was totally cream-crackered).

The Great Meat Riot - 1792: The Shambles, Nottingham Market Place. Because the butchers were charging an absolute fortune for meat a great mob of Nottinghamsters chased them out of the Shambles, nicked their meat then made a bonfire out of doors and books which they 'danced around like savages' (nothing changes much, does it?).

The Great Bread Riot - 1812: Yes, you guessed it.

The Chartist Riot - 1831 - Nottingham, Colwick and Beeston: A Charter to give ordinary folk more voting power was rejected in Parliament so the poor people of Nottingham went nuts, burning down Nottingham Castle, Colwick Hall and a Beeston lace factory because they belonged to 'anti-chartists'.

The Poachers' Punch-up 1851 - Rufford Woods: Armed with sticks and stones, forty poachers from Mansfield and Sutton-in-Ashfield battled with ten gamekeepers from the Rufford Estate. In the scrap, one gamekeeper was killed when a rock fractured his skull (boy, how those pheasants cheered!). Later some poachers were arrested and hanged.(so the pheasants cheered some more)

The Race Riot - 23rd August 1958: A huge riot involving at least 1,000 people in which white 'teddy-boys' fought with West Indian immigrants in St Ann's, Nottingham. The following night another massive crowd of teddy-boys gathered, armed with bicycle chains, knives, razors and bottles, hoping for more 'bother'. The West Indian people sensibly stayed away, so the disappointed 'teds' set about stabbing and slashing each other.

Grisly Nottinghamshire is such a lively and interesting place, isn't it? And it's not just lively because of things like rowdy riots. Hundreds of fascinating, and some slightly nutty, characters have lived in the county, and still do. Here are three of them ...

YOU COULD HAVE HEARD A PIN DROP

In 1765, 6-year-old Kitty Hudson of Arnold went to live with her granddad at St Mary's church in Nottingham. It was Kitty's job to sweep the church floor and pick up pins which had fallen off lady's dresses. To keep her hands free for sweeping, Kitty would pop the pins in her mouth. This habit, (combined with a shortage of stripy toothpaste) had a serious effect on her little gnashers and eventually the poor mite ended up completely toothless. But worse was to follow! At the age of 18 Kitty had trouble sleeping and suffered numbness in her legs and arms. So, in 1783, she went to Nottingham General Hospital where, the doctors were left speechless when they discovered that she was positively bristling with pins (you could have heard a pin drop). Yes, instead of putting the pins in the bin, Kitty had been swallowing them and now, her stomach, feet, legs, chest, and all the rest of her, was full of them! Quick sharp, the doctors set about removing the pins (possibly with the aid of an enormous magnet) and in 1785 she was discharged, completely pin-free. Six months later the 'Pin Lady' of Arnold as she was now known, married her childhood sweetheart ('Chip'?) and got a job carrying letters from Nottingham to Arnold twice a day (heaven knows what she did with her elastic bands). She also went on to have 17 children (all of whom were said to be extremely sharp-witted)

DIG THIS!

The 5th Duke of Portland (1800-1879) talks about his extremely weird home

Welcome to my world. I'm a very rich man. But I'm also a very shy man. So I live underground! Here on my country estate, Welbeck, in Nottinghamshire, I've had subterranean rooms and 15 miles of gas-lit tunnels dug out. I've got underground libraries, an underground billiards room, an underground riding school and an underground railway! I eat a roast chicken every day so my cook pops it in a heated carriage and off it tootles along the track to my underground dining room. I've also got an underground dance hall, big enough for 2,000 people. But I haven't held any dances. I'm far too shy! Giggle, giggle! I've got double letterboxes on every door, too. One for in, and one for out! That's because I hate coming face-to-face with my servants. We just post each other notes. Tee hee! Of course, I didn't build my hidey-hole. 15,000 builders and miners from my coal pits did. But I paid them well! And I gave every one of them a donkey and an umbrella! Do you know what? Some people say I'm batty!

LORD MIDDLETON'S 'NOSY PARKER!'

Lord Middleton had a seven mile wall built around Wollaton Park, just high enough to stop anyone peeping in. One day he was infuriated to spot someone looking over the wall and checking out his estate so he immediately ordered another course of bricks to be added for the entire 7 miles of the wall's length. Some time later he discovered that the 'nosey-parker' had been a giant from Goose Fair taking his morning stroll. Ha!

Chapter Ten

BATTERED AND BOMBED ... BUT NOT BEATEN NOTTINGHAMSHIRE DURING THE WORLD WARS

Nottinghamshire has been through two world wars and survived them. But not without some spine-chilling and grisly goings-on!

Ten very grisly facts about ...

THE HUMONGOUS GREAT CHILWELL EXPLOSION OF 1918

1) World War One was raging. The Germans were pounding tens of thousands British soldiers to bloody pulp in the trenches of France with their vastly superior shells. We had to match them at their own game.

2) It was decided to build an enormous shell factory at what was then the tiny village of Chilwell in Nottinghamshire. 10,000 women were set to work at the factory because the poor blokes were all busy being blasted to bits in France.

3) The women worked 12 hour shifts, 6 days a week, filling shells with deadly poisonous explosive and being paid a measly 30 shillings (£1.50) a week for their efforts.

4) As they worked, the women complained of chest pains, sickness and skin irritations. They were given masks to protect them from the toxins.

5) The masks did no good and eventually, because of all the poisonous gunk they were handling, the women's hair turned green and their skin went yellow! As a result, these unlucky girls became known as the 'Chilwell Canaries'.

6) But worse was to come. On 1st July 1918, a whopping great 8 tons of TNT exploded, blowing the factory and workers sky high. No one's sure why this happened. It could have been set off by enemy saboteurs or it may simply have been an accident.

7) The blast was so powerful that it was heard 30 miles away in the Vale of Belvoir and broke the windows in the village of Long Eaton, 2 miles away.

8) 137 workers were killed and 250 were injured. Body parts were hurled high into the air, many of them landing in nearby farmers' fields.

9) The bodies of the 137 dead were so badly mutilated that only 32 could be identified. The rest were laid to rest in a mass grave at nearby Attenborough without being named.

10) The British government kept the disaster a secret, only allowing the newspapers to say that 60 people had been killed in a factory explosion in the Midlands. In truth, it was the most devastating explosion of World War One, killing more people in one terrible moment. Even more than in the explosions on the battlefields of France.

Not many people know this ...

HOW THE ROUGHNECKS OF WYOMING CAME TO OLD SHERWOOD FOREST AND SAVED BRITAIN FROM DISASTER

A spine-chilling situation: 1942 - World War Two was raging. Britain's cities had been blasted and battered by two years of German bombing, food was short, the British army had been walloped by the Germans, Hitler's forces were controlling most of Western Europe. The people knew they were in terrible danger!

And a spine-chilling secret! But the government knew something else. The British people were in far, far more danger than they actually realised.

What was this spine-chilling secret? Britain was almost out of oil! The tankers bringing vital supplies were being blown out of the sea by the enemy and German bombing raids were turning oil storage tanks into blazing infernos. We now had only a few weeks supply left.

Should we do the unthinkable? Oil was desperately needed for fuelling fighter planes, cargo ships, fighting ships, munitions factories, tanks, lorries and dozens more things that the nation's survival depended on. It was looking very much like the British government would now actually have to surrender to Hitler and his hated Nazis!

An astonishing last-minute revelation: But then, just when it seemed that all was lost, an oil man revealed an astonishing fact. There were huge quantities of oil under Nottinghamshire's Duke's Wood at Eakring, a remnant of the Old Sherwood Forest, near Newark-on-Trent. Enough to save the day! But there was a problem! It needed to be got out of the ground very quickly! And we just didn't have the 'know-how'.

The solution: The cry went up: 'Send for the Yanks! Their 'roughnecks' have been drilling oil in places like Texas, Oklahoma and Wyoming for yonks.' And the roughnecks (as the oil workers were known) came, bringing their drilling rigs with them.

No one must know! But the roughnecks' presence had to be kept secret so the Nazis didn't find out about the vital oilfield and bomb it. So, when they weren't drilling oil, they were hidden away with the monks in nearby Kelham Monastery.

It worked! Soon, no less than 450 oil wells were pumping millions of barrels of oil from Duke's Wood and the nearby Nottinghamshire villages of Caunton, Eakring and Kelham. Oil that would not only save Britain from its terrible predicament but would also be used to fuel the 'D Day' invasion of Nazi-held France that would eventually lead to the defeat of Hitler.

Something to do

Visit the Duke's Wood Oilfield and its wonderful little museum, check out the graffiti carved on a tree by the roughnecks back in 1943 and marvel at their last remaining 'nodding-donkey' oil rig.

BOMBS IN OUR BACKYARD

EXTRACTS FROM THE WORLD WAR TWO DIARY OF MILLY FISHPOOL AGE 9 NEWARK GIRL AND DESCENDANT OF MARMADUKE FISHPOOL (1605-1646)

1st September 1939 Mum has just told me that that the horrible German bloke called Hitler has invaded Poland and it will mean big trouble for everyone here. We aren't allowed to have lights at night. It's called the black out.

3rd September 1939 Today we declared war on Germany*. I wonder what it is going to be like. (*not just our family, all the country)

February 1940 The skies around Newark are full of roaring aircraft endlessly taking off and landing at all the Royal Air Force airfields what are round here.

September 1940 Some kids from Newark what were sent to Canada for safety got torpedoed in their ship. I'm glad I stayed home.

January 1941 They have built big air raid shelters in Newark. Me and my friend Joyce had a peep in one. And guess what! There was a bloke and his girlfriend in there, kissing! A lad off our street called Fred has been taken away by the police for pinching lightbulbs out of them.

Saturday 8th March 1941 Yesterday was the most TERRIFYING thing I have ever had in my life! First I was woken air up by raid sirens going then machine guns firing BLAT BLAT BLAT! like that. I looked out the window and saw a German bomber come out of the clouds and dive at the ball-bearing factory across the street from us. It was dropping bombs. BOOM! BOOM! BOOM! they went! There was smoke and flames everywhere and screaming hurt people all over the place, then police and people and my Mum and Dad rushing to help the factory workers who were blown up. But as they were dragging them out of the wreckage another bomber came and dropped 5 more bombs. Luckily only one exploded but now I am dead scared that soon we will ALL be blown to smithereens!

Sunday 9th March 1941 Mum has just told me that 40 people got killed in the raid on the ball bearing factory and 165 got wounded. All our windows got smashed too and Albert Green's lovely little dog, Laddy, has had to be put down because he got a shrapnel piece in his head.

August 1941 Another terrible thing today. A British bomber plane has crashed on a house killing 6 little kids who were asleep in it. Their dad was working on the railway and saw it happen but he didn't know that it was his own house what got destroyed and he just carried on working! What a terrible, terrible shock that poor man must have had when he got home.

7th May 1945 Hurrah! It's over. We have beaten the Germans good and proper! We are going to have a massive party in our street because we are so HAPPY! But I still can't stop thinking about poor little Laddy and those 6 kids what were got killed in their own house and those friends of me mum and dad killed in the ball-bearing factory.

So that's it – a tour round some of the most grisly bits of Nottinghamshire's history. But even that isn't everything that's sickly, putrid or downright unpleasant about Nottinghamshire. I haven't even mentioned the Loutish Luddites or the monster in the River Trent... perhaps another time. In the meantime, why not join your local library and borrow some books on Nottinghamshire history and see if you can find more grisly things.